PEACE SUTRA

THE ARCHIVED ANCIENT WISDOM SERIES

DR HANISH SHARMA

This book is dedicated to

His Divine Grace A.C. Bhaktivedanta Swami Prabhupad

Founder Acarya of

International Society for Krsna Consciousness

(ISKCON)

Contents

Acknowledgements

This book won't be complete if i dont thank few very important people.

My parents - Sh.Nilamber Sharma and Smt. Gurminder Sharma.

It is because of them, what I am today.

They told me stories and also gave me all the reading material that I ever asked for.

A big hug and thanks to my wife, Dr Richa Verma (MD) who is the also co-author of this book. She cooperated with me while I was busy writing this book.

She is my first critic and always gives useful inputs from time to time that help shape my lectures and talks.

I would like to pay my respect unto the feet of His Grace Raghunath Prabhu and Her Grace Raspriya Mata g who gave direction to my spiritual life.

I had no idea what to do with my queries. They showed me the way.

Love to my kids, Hari and Nimai, who tolerated my absence while I was doing research for this book.

And the beginning, the middle, the end and everything in between I thank the almighty for blessing me with the strength to bring this dream to a reality.

FOREWORD

HAPPY READERS AND SATISFYING REVIEWS

Enlightening ?

"This book is beautiful combination of ancient wisdom along with modern insights . 'Peace Sutra' is must recommended for anyone interested in personal growth, mindfulness & spiritual development ?"

A fantabulous book ??

"I highly recommend this book as it has all u know and all u want to know. This book is perfect for a person thirsty for spiritual knowledge."

The book is really helpful for life lessons

"It felt really good reading the book, it was awsmm. It is for lifetime. Author really searched a lot writing this book."

Worth reading

"In this book the author pens down all the qualities which one can imbibe in oneself to bring peace to one's mind and soul,in a very interesting way,supporting his point with some very interesting and untold stories from puranas. The author very successfully holds our interest till the end .Highly recommended for all age groups. Looking forward to read more of his work."

Amazing

"Its really well written. All the stories narrated in the books are heart touching and seems very practical to follow in our daily life. The book has the ability to hold the reader till the end. Great work. May you keep writing many more books and one more thing this book is such which even children will find easy to read and adapt."

Inspiring and unique style of writing ✍....

"I learnt so much from this book ?, I can't wait to read more of your (Dr Hanish's-author) work......Every story with so many moral values much much required in today's world for people to understand and apply in their lives. Yes it's definitely a Book for all ages. Go for it...Message through this book forms the core of our society."

Read it in one go....

It's a book which I read in one go...I was not able to keep the book down while reading..It's a lovely knowledgeable book for all age groups especially children as ancient stories are linked to morals .Very easy to understand.Keep it up Dr Hanish and Dr Richa.

Preface

One more book on wisdom? Aren't there too many already? What new is left to offer?

Just twisting and re-modelling words and presenting the same old thing with a new title and cover....... like so many are doing.

Fiction writing would have been a better option.

These were my thoughts and concerns as I started writing this book.

But somewhere deep down we all know that even after reading and practicing the fundamentals mentioned in *all* these books, there is a dearth of peace, a scarcity of happiness and ever rising emotional desolation. *Why?*

When I was a child, I was always inspired by stories (I think we all are) - Stories, told by my mother, father, grandparents and teachers.

And the greatest impact comes from the stories that are compiled in our scriptures like Ramayana, Mahabharata and other books of ancient wisdom. The impression those tales left on my young mind, helped laying a strong foundation of my personality and shaping my future.

So coming to the question of .... *why this book?*

With the progress of modern era, we are slowly forgetting what made the core of our society, the basis of our heritage. *The books that made us what we are - the greatest civilastion of all times.*

Despite so many aggressions and assaults by the foreign invaders, we stood tall and resisted being impugned. We rose again from the ashes every time we were burnt to the ground; coming back stronger every time we were defeated.

All this because of the strong foundation laid by our scriptures.

This book series *'Books are the basis'* will bring to you the hidden gems of our glorious ancestorage along with life lessons that I have lived myself and tried successfully on my patients over the past 11 years of my practice in medical profession.

Not keeping you long from this nectar, I bring to you the first book in this series 'Peace Formula'.

This book is a result of extensive research and hard work.

With blessings and love from all you lovely readers, I am sure many more books will come.

Enjoy the ride in the rich history of our nation.

You will find that truth is far more interesting and enlightening than fiction.

Yours Truly
Dr Hanish Sharma

I

Parents are the visible gods. Keep them happy.

Ever heard this quote before?

Though spoken many times by atheistic people in an attempt to replace worship of God, this statement is true, if not used in comparison.

There is one God and there are many gods. And our parents are definitely among them. Whatever greatness we hold today is all because of them.

Growing up we become so many things. One of them is being ungrateful.

Lack of gratitude takes away our peace and we feel agitated, knowing little that simple effort of making gratitude a habit, can bring so much comfort to our mind.

And what better way to start this practice, then to be grateful towards our parents, who actually deserve it. By keeping them happy we get the blessings of God, we gain from their life long experience, what to talk of their unconditional love and emotional support.

So here is a beautiful story from Srimadbhagvatam puran that re-emphasises this basic principle. Remember, it is a true story that actually happened.

Enjoy!

KING NABHAG AND THE WEALTH OF THE SAINTS
(From Srimadbhagvatam Puran)

Long ago, there ruled a king named Nabhag. The youngest son of Nabhag named Nabhaaga lived for a long time at the place of his spiritual master. Therefore, his brothers thought that he was not going to become a grihastha and would not return.

It was not very uncommon in those times for young boys to adopt brahmcharya as the way of their lives and lead a life full of spiritual awakening and in pursuit of higher purpose.

Consequently, without providing a share for him, they divided the property of their father among themselves.

When Nabhaaga returned from the place of his spiritual master, they gave him their father as his share. They were full of treachery and wanted to cheat their brother.

Nabhaaga inquired, "My dear brothers, what have you given to me as my share of our father's property?"

His elder brothers answered, "We have kept our father as your share."

But when Nabhaaga went to his father and said, "My dear father, my elder brothers have given you as my share of property,"

The father replied, "My dear son, do not rely upon their cheating words. I am not your property."

Father is the seed giver. He is the one who implants the child in mother's womb. How can he be a property?

Nabhaag's brothers here are depicting the typical cheating mentality of the people around us. Greatest of relations are maligned just over some land or wealth. Years of siblings love goes down the drain over disputes of inheritance.

Nabhag was very learned and as a past king he was aware of what was going on in his kingdom. In compassion for his simple hearted son, he decided to help him to make means for his livelihood.

Nabhag said: "Far from here, there is a place where all the descendants of Angira rishi are now going to perform a great fire sacrifice (a yajna). Although they are very intelligent, on every sixth day they will be bewildered in performing sacrifice and will make mistakes in their daily duties. Go to those great souls and describe two Vedic hymns pertaining to Vaisvadeva. This will remove their imperfection and help in fulfilment of their sacrifice."

He continued: "When the great sages have completed the sacrifice and are going to the heavenly planets, they will give you the remnants of the money they have received from the sacrifice. Therefore, go there immediately."

Thus Nabhaaga acted exactly according to the advice of his father. The great sages were very happy on being rectified and on completion of their sacrifice. They gave Nabhaaga all their wealth and then went to the heavenly planets.

Thereafter, while Nabhaaga was accepting the riches, a black-looking person from the north came to him and said, "All the wealth from this sacrificial arena belongs to me."

Imagine, all the travel, all the hard work, and not being able to collect your reward. I deserve it. Why can't I have it? This is so unfair. All those thoughts dint trouble him. He had his inner peace with him.

Nabhaaga then said, "These riches belong to me. The great saintly persons have delivered them to me."

When Nabhaaga said this, the black-looking person replied, "Go to your father and ask him to settle our disagreement. Whatever he says let me know"

Nabhaaga was a man of principles. His training at his Guru's ashram had not gone in vain. In accordance with this scenario,

Nabhaaga inquired from his father.

The father of Nabhaaga said: "Whatever the great sages sacrificed in the arena of the Daksa-yajna, they offered to Lord Shiva as his share. Therefore, everything in the sacrificial arena certainly belongs to Lord Shiva. The person you met, who claims this wealth, is no other but Lord Shiva himself.

Nabhaaga went back and offered obeisances to Lord Shiva.

Nabhaaga said: "O worshipable lord, everything in this arena of sacrifice is yours. This is the assertion of my father. Now, with great respect, I bow my head before you, begging your mercy."

Lord Shiva manifested in his beautiful form and said: "Whatever your father has said is the truth, and you also are speaking the same truth. You could have lied to me. But you were never affected by greed and stayed by the virtues of honesty."

Shiva continued "I am pleased by your actions. Therefore, I, who know the Vedic mantras, shall explain transcendental knowledge to you"

He smilingly instructed, "Now you may take all the wealth remaining from the sacrifice, for I give it to you."

After saying this, Lord Shiva, who is most adherent to the religious principles, disappeared from that place.

Lord Shiva is ashutosh, the one who is most easily pleased. He is unattached to the worldly attractions, leads a simple life himself, but provides his followers with all the benedictions, comforts and worldly riches. To those seeking spiritual enlightenment, he shows them the path of pure devotional service.

With this wealth and his father's wisdom, Nabhaaga became king Nabhaaga and ruled the kingdom for many years and his empire flourished with peace and prosperity.

It is mentioned in scriptures, if one hears and chants or remembers this narration in the morning and evening with great attention, he certainly becomes learned, experienced in understanding the Vedic hymns, and expert in self-realization.

∾

Parents are the visible gods. Keep them happy.

Love your parents and treat them with loving care. For you will only know their value when you see their empty chair." –Anonymous

Abraham Lincoln said "All that I am, or hope to be, I owe to my mother."

So be grateful. Respect and love your parents. They have always been there for us. And when we reciprocate, we get inner peace. Once we imbibe this feeling in our heart, the journey to peace begins. The stability we always needed comes by itself.

These days, so many stand-up comedians make fun of their parents in their acts. For them I want to say, if you believe what you are saying, you may get a laugh, but you will not get peace.

Your parents are your greatest asset. Touch their feet. Take their blessings. Make them smile. It can create wonders.

৪৩

II

Be Self-LESS to become Stress-LESS

"Give, and it will be given to you. A good measure, pressed down, shaken together and running over, will be poured into your lap. For with the measure you use, it will be measured to you."

Luke 6:38; **Bible: New International Version (NIV)**

Sharing is caring- one of the first life lessons I taught my sons. Being the younger sibling, I too learnt it quite early from my sister with whom

I shared everything. And most of the times, it was a joy.

In today's era when the competition is cut throat, where you have to step on others head to rise in this portentous struggle to survive, being selfless seems a little obsolete.

What will I get in return? Will the other person reciprocate accordingly? What if he doesn't?

And thus begins the turmoil - a discommode that interrupts our peaceful existence.

To part with something that you love or something for which you worked hard is not easy. But so is attaining peace.

Let us ruminate on this pastime as told by Lord Brahma himself that emphasises on giving. stay tuned.

PARVATI AND THE CLUTCH OF THE CROCODILE (From Brahma Puran)

It all began with the desire of the king of all mountains, Himvan (we call as Himalaya) to be among the most respected and famous personalities in the world.

When he enquired this from Kashyap Muni, he was told that a great progeny can glorify the name of his parents.

So he should perform severe austerities unto Lord Brahma and ask for an exalted daughter who would bring laurels to his lineage.

And so it happened. Pleased with Himvan's worship, Brahma gave him the benediction of such daughter.

He told Himvan that many places of pilgrimage will reside in Himalayas and he will be worshippable even by the demigods.

In due course of time, from his wife Maina, a beautiful daughter was born. She was named Parvati as she was daughter of a mountain (parvat).

Surprisingly she stopped eating anything and just focussed on her meditation. She was called Aparna (one who doesn't even eat leaves or leafy vegetables).

Her mother being aggrieved from her not eating anything said "Dear daughter, don't do this" which in Sanskrit means 'u' 'ma' ('don't' 'do' 'this'). So she was named Uma.

The whole planetary system and the inhabitants became aggrieved with the heat of her rigorous austerities.

Brahma had to come himself to intervene. He said "Dear daughter, why are you troubling whole of the creation? In your eternal form, you are the creator, why you want to destroy what you have created yourself? You have everything you want. What else do you want to achieve with this austerity?"

Parvati replied "Respected Lord, nothing is hidden from you. You know what I want. Then why do you ask me?"

Brahma said "Whom you desire, will come to you himself. Lord Shiva is the greatest husband in this world and he will come and accept you as his wife. I and all demigods are like servant to him."

This was re-instated by demigods who were present there. They requested Parvati to stop further austerities and she obliged.

One day when she was standing in her garden, a dark complexioned dwarf sage came who was no taller than an arm's length. His face was distorted and he had a hunchback. His nose was cut and his hair were dry, pale and lacking any lustre.

He said "Dear lady, I want to marry you"

Parvati with all her aggregated piety could realise that this dwarf was no other than Lord Shiva himself. She worshipped him with a welcome drink and mouth freshner and said "O Lord, I am not independent of my parents. Please talk to my father. Only he has the right to give me in marriage."

Shiva in that distorted form went to Himvan and proposed to marry his daughter. Himvan being unable to recognise the true identity of this dwarf became terrified. But he couldn't refuse directly as he was afraid to get cursed by the sage.

Himvan said "I don't want to disrespect you, my Lord. But I had long back decided to give my daughter in swyamvar (a gathering of aspiring kings and other men from which the girl has the right to choose her own husband in father's presence). It is her own sweet will, whoever she wants to choose."

Dwarf returned to Parvati and told her all this.

He said "Your father is arranging for a swyamvar. All sorts of handsome men will be coming there. Why would you choose me over them?"

Parvati replied "I will choose you only. And if you have any doubts, I accept you here only as my husband."

She picked up a garland of Ashoka tree leaves and put it on the shoulder of the dwarf and accepted him as her husband. The Ashoka tree, being instrumental in their marriage, was blessed by the sage to be perennial tree and a bestower of all blessings.

After this, the dwarf bade goodbye. Soon he was gone and Parvati sat there on a rock meditating on her husband.

Just then she heard a sharp cry from a nearby pond. It was the cry of a young child. A young boy had fallen in water and a crocodile was trying to pull him deeper with his sharp teeth.

Child shrieked "Someone please save me. I have been caught by this crocodile and I am about *to faint. I won't survive much longer. Please help me."*

Parvati rushed to that place. She saw this beautiful child partly in the mouth of the crocodile trying to come out. His whole body was shaking due to fear. Every time the croc pulled him down, he let out a deafening cry. Parvati was filled with agony to see this.

She said "O king of crocodiles! Please leave this child. Please do not kill him."

He replied "My dear lady! I take meal on every 6th day of the fortnight. Whatever Lord sends on my way on this day, I eat it and stay alive. So I can't let him go."

Parvati pleaded "I have done a lot of austerities. Please accept the fruit of all my piety and let him live. I pay my obeisances to you."

Crocodile said "Sure. I accept it and the child will be freed. But beware; you did these austerities for a purpose. Once you donate its fruit to me, you will be bereft of the benediction you got. You will lose all the blessings you have received."

In front of Parvati's eyes, the croc turned golden and effulgent like a sun. It was even difficult to look at him; such was the impact of Parvati's penances.

He continued "It is not easy to accumulate so much spiritual wealth that you have donated just to save this child. I am pleased with your actions. It is really difficult to give up your wealth like this. Please accept it back. I won't harm the child too."

Parvati said "O Crocodile! What to say of my austerities, even if I had to give my life to save this child, I would have happily given. This action of mine was well thought of. I can perform austerities again. So you keep this effulgence and the benefits, which I have already donated to you. I won't take it back."

Parvati showed selfless conviction and unflinchingly stood by her words. The crocodile and the child disappeared from her vision. As she sat down to start her austerity again, Lord Shiva appeared.

Lord Shiva said "My Dear Parvati! Please don't do any more penances. I was the crocodile and I was the child. I just wanted to see how selfless you were and to what extent you would go to help someone in distress. I am very pleased with your actions. You gave your effulgence to me only. Hence I am returning it back to you. It will be multiplied thousand times and will never perish."

Parvati was very happy and started eagerly waiting for the swyamvar. So the day came. The palace was decorated beautifully. Himvan had made announcements everywhere.

Great personalities like Brahma's many sons, Indra (the god of heaven), Agni (the god of fire), Kuber (the treasurer of demigods), Chandrama (the moon god) and Ashwini Kumar (the most beautiful twin gods) all had come hoping to marry Parvati.

Little did they know that Parvati was no other than Sati, the eternal wife of Lord Shiva, who in her previous life had left her body to protest the insult of her husband done by her father, Daksha.

All were eagerly waiting for Parvati to arrive and choose her husband. Parvati came. To everyone's surprise there appeared a small baby in her lap.

How could a maiden girl, yet to choose her husband, be holding a baby? And what else, she smiled at the baby and started turning back from the wedding arena.

This was not tolerated by the demigods who one by one tried to attack the child. Just as they moved forward with an intention to release their weapon, their hands and in turn their whole body was frozen. They could not move even an inch. Seeing such scenario, Brahma realised that the baby was no other than Lord Shiva himself.

He said addressing the baby "My dear Lord! Your pastimes are unparalleled and out of the *imagination of ordinary beings. Please forgive us for not being able to recognise you sooner."*

He then said addressing Indra and other demigods "You all are big fools. You don't know, the baby is Lord Shankar (another name for Shiva) himself. Surrender unto him."

All demigods were frozen. They couldn't move. So they surrendered mentally and offered their obeisances in the mind. Lord Shiva appeared in his natural form and blessed them all. All were relieved to have their bodies moving again. Brahma offered to perform marriage rituals of Shankar-Parvati.

Thus, the eternal couple came together again for the benefit of whole humanity.

৪৩

Be Self-LESS to become Stress-LESS

Swami Vivekananda said "He who has more of this unselfishness is more spiritual and nearer to Shiva. Truth, purity, and unselfishness —

wherever these are present, there is no power below or above the sun to crush the possessor thereof."

Isn't it worth a try?

Living for one's own self and selfish motives is a life even lesser than animals. Even they also work selflessly when it comes to work for some higher actions.

As long as we act miserly, we tend to attract the negativity. We fail to absorb the magnanimity of Mother Nature. But once we start giving back, more than we take, we start on this path of selflessness. We let go what was binding us, holding us back and we invoke the inner peace.

Just like Parvati was ready to give up her life and all that was valuable to her just to save one life, we should also be ready to sacrifice our attachments for the greater purpose.

We may not be able to imitate her. But we can definitely follow on her footsteps.

Think about it.

III

Running after Fame, Ruins the Name

Albert Einstein said" With fame I become more and more stupid, which of course is a very common phenomenon."

FAME – The most desired attribute, a desire that has become a necessity. Social media approval, craving for likes, hunger for views, and the never ending want for subscribers.

Happy faces, crying souls is the apt description of most social media influences these days.

In a journey to achieve the unachievable, we fall down and lose the most precious gift, given to us by the almighty: inner peace.

Once Ramanand Rai, a great scholar of 16th century was asked by Sri Chaitanya Mahaprabhu, incarnation of Lord Krishna and Radharani's combined form, about the greatest fame in the world.

Ramanand Rai replied "The greatest fame is to be known as a devotee of the Lord."

Even with a neutral mind, is fame really the solution to all our problems?

Indeed it solves some problems but creates many more, just like beheading the head of the demon king Ravana.

Peace and fame rarely go the same way. The momentary happiness that we get because of name and fame ruins our eternal peace.

In the end, it all boils down to our choice. Are we sure, what we want? Do we really want that *stability and happiness in our life?*

Or we want to keep on running behind fame, just like a dog running after a car. He may never catch it. Even if he catches it, he will never be able to drive.

Stop looking at fame the way the society and social media projects it. And the biggest irony is those who don't want it and work hard in silence, get it the most often.

Quoting a dialogue in a Bollywood movie "Kamyabi ke peeche mat bhaago, kamyab bano, kamyabi khud tumhare peeche ayegi" "Don't run after success, become able and competent, success will come after you."

Sharing a small story from Vaman Puran which might change the way you look at the things.

See you at the other side of this true story.

৪০

THE MOUNTAIN THAT REFUSED TO BOW (From Vaman Puran)

There existed a time when Himalayas were not the king of the mountains and Mt Everest was not the tallest peak. The crown was held by Vindhyachal Mountain range.

Vindhya, the person form of Vindhyachal Mountains, was very proud. He stood tall and looked upon everyone else as small and puny. His beautiful peaks were always adorned with snow, shining on its own. Lower parts supported many forms of vegetation and a rich diversity of animal life. His tallest peaks reached far above the clouds and even dared to obscure the sun light.

The Sun with all its might could not pass from above. To sustain life on other side of the mountains, he had to go all the way around the Vindhya. And it was a cumbersome task, even for the Sun God. Such was the magnanimity of Vindhyachal.

One day, Sun God approached Vindhya.

He said "O King of mountains! I want to make a request to you. Please listen to it with calm mind. You are so tall and huge. Your name is known to inhabitants of all the heavenly planets. But for residents on your western side, it is becoming difficult to survive."

He continued "As I have to go all the way round you, to reach your western side, it causes delay and sometimes I am not able to give them shade for the required time. So in the benefit of all humanity, I request you to reduce your height. And let me pass directly above you as I do over other mountains."

Vindhya replied "I am not going to bow down to anyone. I am not the king for no reason. Whole world knows my name. They call me king of the mountains. And you want me to bow down? I will tell you what. Now you won't be able to even go around me with ease. I won't let you ruin by name and be looked down as the one who bowed down."

This attitude of Vindhya was known to all. They called his name as the king of mountains. But in their hearts they had no love and respect for him. Simple disgust and disdain due to his towering ego and false pride. Greater he wanted to become, the lesshet became. He was bereft of the blessings of the sages and in the end was all alone in the journey of his life.

Sun was disappointed. In this gloomy state of mind, he felt helpless and had no idea what to do.

Just then the great sage Agastya rishi was passing by. The might of Agastya Muni was known to all. He once drank the whole ocean like one drinks a glass of water. Sun saw a ray of hope.

He bowed down to Agastya rishi and said "O learned sage! It is my utmost fortune that you have come here. I am in despair and its only you who can help me. The might of Vindhyachal is becoming an agony for those living on its western side and me as their well-wisher. I requested him to bow down a little but he has refused blatantly rather he has threatened me. I take shelter of your feet. Please bless this servant of yours."

Agastya Rishi felt merciful. The request of Surya got him thinking, how to tackle the pride of Vindhya. He thought of a way. He went to Vindhyachal.

Vindhyachal was surprised to have such a powerful visitor. He paid obeisances with his words and asked the rishi purpose of his visit.

Agastya Rishi said "Dear Vindhyachal! I am travelling to south India and for that I have to cross you. I know you are very tall and known for your grandiosity. But understand my situation. I am getting old. I don't have the same strength and agile that I had many years back."

He continued "I need your help. If you could reduce your height and keep it that way till I am back. It would be easier for me to cross and come back. I won't take long. And you will be eternally known for this good deed of yours."

Vindhya was not sure. But he also did not want to enrage the powerful ascetic. Half-heartedly, he agreed and slowly bent down. This was the first time in the history that such thing ever happened. All demigods watching from the sky showered flowers upon Agastya Rishi and Vindhyachal.

Agastya Rishi went and never came back. Vindhyachal stayed like that and is still sitting bowed down in wait of Agastya Rishi.

Did Agastya rishi lie? No! He said he will come back soon. As compared to our eternal life, even few million years are soon only. He had never intended to come back in many yugas to come. But for the benefit of humanity he decided to trick Vindhya.

And it was a win-win for all.

Vindhyachal was known as the mountain that bowed down to a saint. He was not looked down upon, rather he was glorified beyond imagination. All the sages who didn't or couldn't go to Himalayas, stayed in Vindhyachal.

With their blessings, the vegetation, the animal life, the beauty of the hills all increased many fold. And most importantly for Vindhya, he got what he desired.

Those who seek fame may or may not get it. But those who work in silence and let their actions speak are the ones who get an eternal name.

ॐ

Running after Fame, Ruins the Name

Fame is not a necessity nor should it be a desire. As long as we run after fame, we won't be able to achieve peace. If its peace and happiness we seek, we should debug our system from this desire to be known.

We hanker for 3 As – Appreciation, Accumulation and Accomplishment. In very small amounts, these hankerings are not harmful. But we never come to know, when these take control over our consciousness, our actions and in turn the results.

So don't run after fame. Keep the example of Vindhyachal in your mind. He had everything he wanted and that made him proud. He had his name known to some, but when he subdued his ego to a saint and surrendered unto his feet, his name was known to the entire cosmic creation.

He was thinking his name will be ruined by being humble. Instead it rose to an unfathomable height. He got what he truly needed- happiness and blessings.

Choice is yours.... Peace or Fame? Happiness or Name? Ponder upon this. You will realise the depth of this story and the magnitude of this thought.

Moving on.

IV

Nothing to die for,
Nothing to live for

Do you have a higher purpose in your life? How do you define your life till now?

Whatever we do is mainly divided in four categories. Eating, sleeping, mating and defending. Either directly or indirectly – we all are working for that only. All the rivers of our actions end in the ocean of these four goals.

Here is an exercise for you. Take a piece of paper and a pen. Write down five accomplishments in your life that do not fall in

*these four categories. Harder than you think.
Right ?*

Your degree? Your hard earned house? Your ever maintenance requiring family? Your beautiful car? Dependable Social Security? A fit body for which you work out or plan to work out every day?

All the above objects of desire, lie in the above mentioned four categories only. Do you ever think why even after making so much material progress, many people around us are unable to attain simple peace.

They have to take sleeping pills or anxiolytics just to sleep at night. The simplest explanation is lack of purpose. They lack an aim in their life for which they will lay down their lives, at least, laying down their comfort and selfish ulterior motives.

Sharing a story of Vikram and Betaal mentioned in Bhavishya Puran which will make you re-think and re-define your life.

Ready to be amazed?

THE SOLDIER WHO KILLED HIS SON (From Bhavishya Puran)

Long ago in a very rich and prosperous kingdom named Vardhaman lived a king named Roopsen who was a very pious king and generous king. He had a chaste wife whose name was Vidvanmala.

One day in his court a very courageous warrior came. His name was Veerver. He was accompanied by his wife, daughter and son. He had come seeking a job suitable to his skills and talent.

As he described his various previous roles and assignments, King heard patiently. Being impressed with his resume and stories of glory, he offered him a salary of thousand gold coins every month and asked him to guard the main door, Simha dvar, of the palace.

Veerver said "O my Lord! I will always work for the welfare of this kingdom and yourself.

Even if I have to die for this purpose, I won't hesitate."

It was mutually agreed that this would be a temporary appointment which will be permanent after seeing his actions and sincerity. A house was provided to the family in the capital city, not very far from the palace.

When the king enquired from a secret spy, who roamed all around the kingdom and gave various sorts of information to King Roopsen, the King was told that this soldier is very pious. He spends almost all of his salary on donations, serving the poor, serving the devotees, in construction of temples and other pious deeds. He also feeds and clothes orphans. Whatever small amount is left, he uses it to fulfil the needs of his family.

King was very impressed. He made his job permanent and started trusting him completely. Many months passed by like this. Everyone in kingdom was living happily and in great prosperity.

Once, as it happened, in the middle of a black rainy night the clouds were thundering loudly and lightning was shining like it had gone crazy. Wind was blowing so fast, as if the biggest of the trees will be uprooted. The rain and storm were crossing all limits which nobody had ever seen before in that kingdom.

King was resting in his palace room when heard a distant shrill cry of a woman coming from the direction of the cremation ground. This cry turned into a frightening wailing which was not stopping and was heard despite the storm and the thunders.

King called for Veerver and asked him to find out from where this sound was coming. Veerver took his sword and went in the direction of the sound. King also followed him secretively because of the fear of the life of the soldier and to help the soldier, if needed. But the soldier could not see that king was coming behind him. On reaching the burning grounds, Veerver saw a lady crying in that field.

Veerver asked "O lady! Who are you? What are you doing alone in this monstrous night? And why are you crying like this?"

She replied "I am the Rashtra Lakshmi, the money potency of the kingdom, personified. By the end of this month King Roopsen will die. When he will die, I will become an orphan, as he is my maintainer. This Kingdom will lose its wealth and prosperity."

She continued sobbing and said "I am worried, where I will go. What will I do? What will happen to people of this kingdom? These thoughts are disturbing my mind. Because of this, I am crying."

Loyal Veerver asked her "How can our king live long? Please tell me!"

Rashtra Lakshmi replied "There is only one solution. You sacrifice and offer life of your own son's to Chandika Devi. Then king's life can be saved."

This was the life defining moment for Veerver. He had never thought that it would require his son's life to save his king's life. He was always ready to sacrifice his own life, but his young son? What do you think he did?

When the going gets tough, only the tough gets the going. Veerver didn't hesitate. He went back to his home and discussed this with his wife. He brought the family to the temple of Chandika.This entire time king was secretly following him like what he will do. He also had never expected all this to happen.

Veerver entered the temple of Goddess Chandika with his family. He worshipped her, said his prayers and keeping in mind the higher purpose in his life, he took a sword and cut the head of his son in front of the deity of goddess.

This was a horrible and painful site, especially for the younger sister, who could not bear it. She felt so pained at the heart that she died at the spot. Seeing the death of her daughter and her son, the wife of Veerver, also left her body.

Veerver felt sad and deserted. Though he was satisfied that the king and the kingdom will be saved, he was also feeling intense separation from his family. He knew it was his responsibility and he also knew the result of his actions, beforehand.

He believed – if you have nothing to die for, you have nothing to live for. Praying to the goddess with tears in his eyes he picked up his sword and cut his own head, with his own hands.

King was watching. He was afar in the dark. All this happened so fast that he couldn't stop Veerver from giving away his life. While he was watching this, he was amazed as well as shocked to see what all was happening. He could have never even imagined the turn of events.

He bowed before the deity of the goddess. He said his prayers and addressed Goddess Chandika. "O Goddess Chandika! I don't want a long life which came after sacrificing 4 good people. I will kill myself at once. I don't want any of this."

He took a sword and was ready to cut his own head. Immediately the goddess appeared from her deity and held king's hand.

She said "Dear king I am very happy with your actions. You have shown great courage in doing so. Your life is safe and longevity is *confirmed. Apart from that, you can ask for any other boon from me."*

King again bowed before the goddess with utmost humility and tears of compassion in his eyes.

He said "O goddess Chandika! If you are really pleased with my actions and intentions, I request you to please make Veerver and his family alive again. One more request, they may never know that it was because of me that they came back to life."

Like Veerver, king was also never after taking credit. He did not want acknowledgement; he wanted enlightenment. He never wore any attitude; his greatest ornament was his gratitude.

Goddess smiled at his selfless desire. She said "Thata-astu" (yes, it will be true) and then she disappeared. King was very happy and slowly, hiding from the other people of the country, he went back to his palace and lied down.

Veerver woke up as if nothing had happened. He was surprised to see that he and his family members were alive. There was no blood, no wounds and no pain, just the smiling deity of the goddess in front of them. It felt like all of them had woken up from a deep sleep.

He thought for few moments and decided that it must be the mercy of the goddess. She might have got pleased with his actions and spared everyone's life. Night was almost over. Sun could be seen over the horizon. Storm had passed and the sky was clear.

He went back to his home with his family, made them lie down and came back to king's palace and started his guard duty again. Next morning when king Roopsen woke up, he called Veervar.

He asked "Dear Veerver! Who was the lady that was crying last night? Did you get to know what the whole thing was about?"

Veerver replied "My Lord! That must be some Witch who stopped crying as soon as she saw me and she disappeared from the place, not seen again. There is nothing to worry about."

What would have you done if you had done such a heroic act? Most of us would have boasted about it; making King feel thankful towards us, singing our own glories and tales of greatness.

But Veerver chose otherwise. He was a man of actions, not merely hollow words. King was very impressed with Veever's devotion and his loyalty to his master. King was very happy to see such traits in a person, known to him. Such rare qualities were hard to find even in those times, what to talk of today. He decided to marry his daughter to Veerver's son and make him his friend instead of just a palace door guard.

This is a true story as told to king Vikramaditya by Rudrakinkar Betaal. Most of us are familiar with Vikram Betaal stories. Those who don't know I will just give a small introduction.

Betaal was a ghost like creature who occasionally created havoc in the nearby village and then came to rest on a tree. King Vikramaditya went to catch him.

Betaal agreed to be caught, but on one condition, that on the way back King won't speak a word. If he does, Betaal will free himself and go back to some other tree for king to find him out again. Then he used to engage king in some story.

After the story he would ask a question from the king, threatening him that if he would answer incorrectly, his head will burst in thousand pieces. King was very just and pious.

He would answer correctly saving his head from bursting, but Betaal used to fly away as King has broken his own vow of silence. So this pattern happened many times over. So coming back to our story.........

Rudrakinkar Betaal asked the king "You heard the story. Now you have to answer one question. All these people did great unimaginable things because of love for each other. Can you tell me whose love was the highest?"

Betaal continued. "Whether it was
Veerver's love for his master, for whom he
sacrificed his own son or for his family for
whom he sacrificed himself? Or a son's love for
his father who agreed to be slayed in front of
the goddess on his father's instructions? Or a
sister's love for his brother, who couldn't bear
his brother's death and left her body? Or a
mother's love for his children who died on
watching his children die? Or the king's love
for Veerver for whom he was going to severe his
own head, not caring about his own life? Who
among these showed the perfection of true
love?Who actually lived on the principle that if
you have nothing to die for you have nothing
to live for?"

King Vikramaditya replied "All the characters
in this story did their duties perfectly and set
the highest epitome of love. But the love of king
is the greatest among the all."

He continued with gravity in his voice. "Veerver was just a servant of the king and the nation. He got money for his daily services in wages. So that was also a motivation for him to do his service."

"Had he stopped working, he would have stopped getting gold which was one of the primary reasons he joined. So his love and loyalty for his king was unimaginable still was not the highest."

Vikramaditya explained further "Veerver's wife was a chaste and pious lady. Her actions showed her immense love for her husband and her children. The sister also loved his brother a lot. Father loved his family. All these things are great but to some extent natural which can be seen in many good families sharing the bond of love."

He stressed again "But the king Roopsen showed the highest and most ideal love. He was ready to sacrifice his life for a paid servant. This is exceptional."

True. Isn't it?

We won't find easily such examples in entire human history. We may find many examples where people sacrificed themselves for their family. Roopsen's sacrifice and his love for Veerver was the highest. Betaal agreed and he flew away leaving us to ponder upon this story.

&

If we have nothing to die for, we have nothing to live for

Do you have a higher calling in your life? Something- for which you are ready to leave your comfort. Dreams- that don't let you sleep at night. Thoughts- that don't let you think anything but your goal.

Our higher calling defines us. It may be spirituality; it may be social service or doing one simple good deed every day. We can start small, but we should have the desire to make it BIG.

There are two types of people in the world. One are those who come to take from this world.

They are born, they grow, they enjoy, they get old and they die.

And there are others who are born from the womb of the mother; and then they are born again when they realize the purpose of their lives.

Choose to be the second one. You will see miracles happening around you.

Not sure about your calling? Send me a mail. We will find out your higher purpose..... together.

Think about it.

৪০

V

Loyalty is the true Royalty

Some may call this thinking as old school. But the satisfaction of having a loyal partner is one of the greatest feelings of the world. Cheating on or be cheated upon always ends terribly either for one or both and sometimes all involved.

Somewhere the present generation has forgotten this and the condition is worsening with time. One Life, One Wife is no more the life quote of the youth. Live in, having multiple partners, divorce, extra marital relations and domestic violence - these were not heard so often even 20-30 years back, what to talk of ages ago.

Being loyal to someone, who reciprocates the same loyalty and love, uplifts your consciousness to a platform of stability and peace. Ever heard of laminar flow?

"Laminar flow is the property of fluid particles in fluid dynamics to follow smooth paths in layers, with each layer moving smoothly past the adjacent layers with little or no mixing."

When we are honest and loyal, life moves like a laminar flow. Otherwise it is all turbulence. Can't expect peace in turbulence, right?

If you have found someone special in your life and now you are bonded with the sacred bond of marriage or you plan to do that in future, be loyal. Don't go around exploring your options.

Don't seek entertainment as you are bored with your routine monotonous life. Here I am sharing a true story that happened in Sat-Yuga showing the epitome of loyalty, trust and obedience.

This was recorded in Bhavishya Puran as well as Srimadbhagwatam puran, two of the top-most puranas for the science of self-realisation.

Stay with me as I narrate this story. If you have not heard it before, it will keep you on the edge of your seat till the end. And even if you have heard it somewhere, you will love reading it again.

Dive into this historical journey of a princess who was put against all odds, who steered through the storm with her faith and loyalty.

Let's Dive in!

౭

THE MOST DIFFICULT CHOICE (From Bhavishya Puran)

This is the story of a beautiful princess who was forced by the destiny to make the most difficult choices in her life.

In Sat-Yuga there lived a pious king, Sharyati. He along with his family, ministers and whole army had gone to take bath in the sacred waters of river Ganga. For this they chose the banks of the river close to ashram of Chyavan Muni. They all took bath, offered their prayers and offered water to demigods and forefathers.

As they all dressed up again and were ready to go back to the capital city, there was a cry of discomfort and agitation among the army. This cry became louder and louder.

It was a serious matter as the king and ministers too started to feel the discomfort. All of them were experiencing an acute obstruction of the passage of urine and stool. Their abdomens started to distend and slowly their vision was decreasing.

King Sharyati got scared. He shouted loudly "We all are at the pious hermitage of the great ascetic Chyavan Muni. Has anyone committed any offence of any sort? Why this is happening to all of us?" For some time nobody spoke.

Then the beautiful daughter of King Sharyati named Sukanya came forward. She said "My dear father! While I was enjoying the beauty of the nearby forest with my friends, I heard a voice calling my name. We followed the voice. After going some distance deeper in the forest, we saw something fascinating. We saw a tall ant- hill. There were two holes in it from where I could see two glittering lights like some precious stones. I was surprised to see these shining stones in the ant hill."

Sukanya repented "Due to my foolishness and fickleness, I took a thin pointed stick and pierced those shining objects. As soon as I did this, it stopped shining and to my horror blood started coming out. This happened just a few moments ago. Please forgive me father. It is because of me that we all are facing this wrath of nature."

King got aggrieved. He took his daughter along and rushed to the spot. He saw what his daughter had described. Blood was coming out of the two holes in that small mountain of sand.

It was Chyavan Muni himself. He was in a sitting position, meditating for so long that ants had made a hill around him. So absorbed was he in his practice, that he didn't bother ants forming a whole colony around him. The glittering objects that Sunkanya pierced were the eyes of this most powerful sage.

Sharyati Maharaj begged forgiveness "O sage! Please forgive my daughter's offense. She committed this crime in ignorance."

Chyavan Muni woke up from his trance. He replied "It's ok. I have forgiven her. But I will need someone to tend to my needs, so that I can continue my spiritual practices. So I suggest, you marry her to me and leave her to serve me at this hermitage. This will be in her and yours benefit. None of you would have to face the karmic consequences of her action."

King looked at his daughter. After all it was her decision too - The first difficult choice that she had to make.

Chyavan Muni was materially not at all good looking. He was old, wrinkled, had grey hair and was covered with sand from head to toe, whereas Sukanya was the most beautiful princess of that time. He lived in forest. She never in her life had spent even one night out of the comforts of her palace.

It was a huge sacrifice for a mistake committed out of innocence and ignorance. But what could be done now? She had to take a decision. She could either suffer herself or see his father and his army men dying in front of her eyes.

Considering the well-being of his father and his kingdom, she accepted to marry Chyavan Muni and conveyed this to her father. As soon as they accepted the proposal, they became normal again and they had a sigh of relief. King Sharyati married Sukanya with the sage and left the forest, came back to the capital and continued his rule.

Chyavan Muni again started his meditation and went into state of samadhi. Sukanya was brought up well by her parents. They had given her the right teachings and examples on how to live an ideal life as per scriptural injuctions. She started serving her husband with whole hearted devotion. She gave up her royal clothes and ornaments. She simple wore a dress that she made out of tree bark and dear's skin.

In this way many months passed. When spring season, the Muni called his wife with a desire to procreate and produce a child.

Sukanya said "My dear husband! I can never refuse any of your desires. But I want to make a request to you. If you could please beautify yourself and come in a young and handsome form, wearing nice clothes and jewellery, then I would be able to accept you in a better way."

Chyavan Muni said "How is that possible? I am old, you can see that. Neither I am good looking nor am I rich like your father to collect things of opulence. How can I become young and handsome with jewellery?"

She replied "You are one of the most powerful sages. You can use the power of your meditation to become anything you want. This is not a big deal for you."

He said "I am not going to waste my ascetic potency just to transform my body into a physically more presentable person. If you cannot accept me this way I will go back to my meditation."

After having said this he went into samadhi again. And there she sat again serving her husband for many more months to come.

One day the two beautiful twin demigods Ashwini Kumar were passing from that place. They saw beautiful Sukanya all alone in the forest collecting wood, flowers and fruits.

Ashwini Kumaras said "O beautiful lady! Who are you? Why are you living alone in this forest?"

Sukanya replied "I am Sukanya, daughter of king Sharyati. My husband Chyavan Rishi is doing his mediation nearby. I live close to him to serve him. Who are you? Please tell."

Kumaras said "We are the doctors of demigods, Ashwini Kumaras. What happiness will you get from this old husband? Choose one of us as your husband."

She said "Please don't say such words. I am a chaste wife. I am already married to Chyavan Rishi. I cannot even think of another man. I will always stay loyal to him and keep on serving him day and night"

She told them the whole story from the beginning. The twin demigods were really impressed by her words.

They said "Okay. Here is an offer. We are the designated celestial doctors. We can make your husband young and handsome. But when he transforms, you will still have to make choice among the three of us, whom you want to marry."

Sukanya said "Please forgive me. But I will always choose my husband only. Moreover, I cannot make any decision without his permission so you will have to ask him."

They agreed to wait till Sukanya comes back after getting permission from her husband. Sukanya went to her husband and told him everything. Agreeing to the offer, Chyavan Muni with his wife, went to the place where Kumaras were waiting.Chyavan Muni had utmost faith and trusted the loyalty of his wife. Faith and Trust make the foundation of any relationship.

Chyavan Muni spoke to the Kumaras "I agree to your terms. Please make me young again. Sukanya is free to choose anyone she wants. I will accept her decision."

Ashwini Kumar held Rishi from both his arms from both the sides and three of them went inside the Ganga river. After some time, they came out. All three of them were looking exactly alike; similar clothes, similar ornaments, similar godly facial features. It was very difficult for Sukanya to find out who her husband was. She seemed bewildered.

She begged "My Lords! I didn't leave my husband even when he was old and ugly. Now, by your mercy, he has become handsome like you. I take shelter of your feet. Please reveal who my husband is. I am unable to identify him. Have mercy on me"

They stood there, all smiling. After all, it was the condition. She had to find out herself. But feeling merciful, they dropped small hints.

She looked carefully. She saw that two of them were not blinking eyes and also they were few inches above the ground, not touching it with their feet. On the other hand, the third one was standing on the ground and was blinking his eyes like any other human being

She joyfully said "The third one is my husband Chyavan Rishi." Then she touched his feet and took blessings from him. As this happened, musical instruments started playing in the sky and flowers showered from the sky.

Chyavan Muni said to the Kumaras "We are grateful to you for your help. How can I repay you? Those who don't return the favour of a good deed, have to go and live in 21 hellish planets. So please tell me, how I can serve you"

Kumaras replied "You can indeed help us. We are demigods but we belong to the doctor class.

So we are not considered very highly among the demigods. That is why when any sacrifice is performed we are not given a part from it."

Chyavan Muni said "So be it. I will make arrangements to fulfil your desire."

After saying this, he bade them good bye and came back to his hermitage with his wife.

One day King Sharyati, with his wife, came to visit her daughter in the forest and he was surprised to see her daughter with a young and handsome man. He got very angry.

He said "You lustful girl! You left your saint husband for this person just for his looks. How could you do this?"

The daughter replied "Dear father! He is the same person Chyavan Muni. I am chaste to him. Please don't be upset." Then she told him the whole story and he was very pleased.

Seeing the right moment, Muni told King Sharyati to prepare for Mahayagya, a great fire sacrifice. King returned to his capital and started collecting various items required for the ceremony.

Chyavan Muni also went with his wife. All great sages were invited to the fire sacrifice. Proper arrangements were made for all demigods to come.

As the sacrifice progressed, one by one all the demigods were coming to accept their part of the offerings.

Indra was sitting there and watching. To his surprise, he saw Ashwini Kumaras coming. It didn't take him long to understand everything.

In deep thunderous voice he spoke "O Muni! These twin gods are merely doctors. They don't deserve a part from the offerings. So I instruct you not to give them anything."

Chyavan Muni was firm. He said "They did a huge favour to me and I owe them. They have come here only because I invited them. I will definitely provide them with offerings of the sacrifice."

Indra said "If you won't listen to me, I will hit you with the most feared weapon in this world, my Vajra"

Muni wasn't scared. He knew what he was doing. He gave the offerings to the twins. Indra got super angry. He picked up his Vajra to kill Muni. Chyavan Muni was watching alertly.

Immediately, with his mystic potencies, he transfixed Indra in that position, as he was done once before by Lord Shiva also. Unable to move, Indra's ego shattered to the ground. Muni completed the yagya and fulfilled his promise to the twin gods. He remained loyal and truthful to his vow without being scared or deviated.

Lord Brahma intervened and requested Muni to release Indra from the spell. Indra could move again. He bowed down to Chyavan Muni and seeked forgiveness for his egoistic behaviour.

Indra said "Now I realise that whole of this arrangement was made by the Supreme Lord to glorify His devotees like you.

He continued "From today onwards, Ashwini Kumaras will also get a part in the offerings of all sacrifices. Also, I give my blessings that whosoever will hear or read this pastime of yours, will get youth and beauty himself."

Indra went back to his kingdom, the heavens. Muni came back with his wife to his hermitage. To Muni's surprise, at the same place, there were beautiful palaces filled with gems, diamonds, gold and other precious items. There were piles of beautiful clothes and various eatable delicacies.

This was the arrangement of Indra. Sukanya and Chyavan Muni were very happy and they praised Indra for his generosity.

Loyalty is the true royalty

"Hold faithfulness and sincerity as first principles." — Confucius

The less heard and even less followed word loyalty is one of the keys to have a good life- a life we all been looking for.

Sukanya could always choose to leave Chyavan Muni.

He might even have allowed it for her happiness.

Chyavan Muni could have broken his vow of helping the twin gods.

But he chose to be loyal and fulfil his promise.

In the end, both Sukanya and Chyavan Muni got what they desired and what they deserved and may be even more than that.

Had they made the other choice, which was much easier and tempting, what would have been the result?

The path of being loyal is not easy.

Sometimes it is filled with sharp stones and thorns.

It may cut, it may bleed. But it will always be worth it.

In the end the loyal one will get the peace, the eternal happiness.

"There's nothing like a really loyal, dependable, good friend. Nothing." — Jennifer Aniston

Wanna bet?

୫

VI

One who serves, becomes the master.

"Life is for service." – Fred Rogers

Now this chapter is going to be somewhat contradictory to the general verdict that we get from modern day motivational speakers/ authors.

They tell you – become the master. They tell you – become the controller. They tell you – take charge of your destiny. They will never tell you – become a servant.

And they don't tell you that the easiest way to achieve peace is to become a humble servant. Confused?

I will explain. When we serve, we invite all the qualities that come with service – humility, mercy, selflessness, gratitude, generosity and many more. All these qualities bring to us the desired peace. And these are delivered to us as a package deal, when we act in the mood of helping and serving.

"Successful people are always looking for opportunities to help others. Unsuccessful people are always asking, 'What's in it for me?'" – Brian Tracy, Author and Motivational Speaker (one of my favourite speakers and authors)

"Happiness is a by-product of an effort to make someone else happy." – Gretta Palmer, Author and Editor

Still not convinced? Read this inspirational story from Brahma puran- a story of love, sacrifice and service Hold your tears. Would you?

Atithi Devo Bhava – Guest is god (From Brahma Puran)

On Brahmagiri mountain lived a very wicked Huntsman. His name and terror had spread everywhere. He used to kill saints, sages, villagers, cows, birds, deers etc. and he did it all with immense pleasure. He was a sinful man full of anger and dishonesty.

In his hands he always carried a net for trapping the poor animal; a bow and arrows hanging on his shoulders His mindset was full of sinful ideas and was always thinking how to hurt people and animals. His wife and his son were also of similar mentality.

One day with his wife's inspiration, he entered inside the deeper part of the dark forest. This part was usually spared by other hunters and gatherers. There he killed many species of deers and birds. Few birds those who he did not kill, he held them alive and put them in a small cage.

In this way after roaming around very far he was coming on his way back to home. Evening had started and it was a beginning of rainy season. Suddenly lightning struck in the sky and dark clouds covered everything visible above him.Strong winds started blowing and hail storms started falling. It seemed like stones were pelting from the sky. He was being hit and it hurt with every stone of ice falling on his head and body.

The wind became stronger and so did the rain and the stones. Due to heavy rain the condition became more and more horrifying. Hunter was walking since long time. He was exhausted and famished. Water was filling up everywhere. The path was not visible. The path, small hill and the small trenches had come to the same level. He was unable to find his way back.

The hunter started thinking in this way "Where should I go? Where can I stay? What can I do? I was like Yamraj, the bestowe of death to all living entities. Today I myself feel that my life will pass away as I am unable to tolerate this rain and stone shower coming from the sky. I am unable to find any tree or cave or any rock shelter that can save my life."

While he was looking, he saw a big tree very close by which was filled with branches, leaves *and flowers. To his relief, he had finally found shelter. He sat down in inhibition, almost lying down. All his clothes were wet. He was shivering.*

He was also worried if his wife and son would have survived such a storm; whether they had shelter or not; whether they got any food or not. At that time Sun completely set and it was dark all around.

On that tree lived a pair of male and female pigeons with their children and grandchildren. They were living on the tree, from many years, free from any fear.

They were completed satisfied and happy. They used to live in a small hollow inside the tree which was completely safe from wind as well as hailstorms and the rain.

As destiny would have it, on the same day, both of them, the husband and the wife pigeon had gone out to bring food for the younger pigeon children.

But due to the storm only the husband could come back and the wife could not come back to the shelter and safety of the home. Unfortunately she was caught by the same Huntsman and he was carrying her in his cage.

Though she was still alive and had not left her body yet, but she was scared and uncertain about her future. The husband was worried thinking about the safety of his wife and the future of his mother less children. The rain was still going strong and it was completely dark.

He looked around. The hollow of the tree looked even hollower without the wife. All these thoughts were disturbing him. He had no idea that the wife was just below that tree in the cage of the Huntsman. The husband started remembering is wife by gloryfying her qualities.

He said loudly "I don't know where my wife has gone. She used to increase my pleasure and auspiciousness in my family. I don't know why she hasn't come yet. She was the creator of religious principles in my home. It was only because of her association that I could perform any spiritual activity. She is the original owner of this body of mine.

He continued "She helped me in achieving anything that anyone could dream of. When I was happy, she would smile seeing me happy and when I was upset she used to cure my disturbance with her words and actions. In giving suggestions, she was my best friend and in following my orders she was the most loving and loyal helper."

"Even the Sun has set but she hasn't return yet. She knew nothing except her husband. Her life resided in me, her husband. I was her only love. She hasn't returned yet. What should I do? Where should I go?"

"My home without her looks like a deserted place, not suitable to live. When she was here even deserted places and scary times looked sweet and homely. Without her, my home is not home."

"I won't be able to live without her. If she has left her body, I will also leave my body. But what my kids will do without her? How will they survive?"

In this way when he was crying, the wife in the cage of the hunter was listening to everything.

She too cried out loudly. "O dear husband! I am helpless. I am caught in this cage. This hunter has captured me. But I am honoured and my life is successful as I am listening to my husband glorifying me as I may leave this body very soon."

"I have no qualities of my own. Whatever qualities I have, only you have given them to me. I am very thankful to you. Today I am utmost grateful. It is said if husband is satisfied from the wife then even the demigods are satisfied from her and on the other hand if the husband is unsatisfied then there is no satisfaction in the life of that lady. Dear husband, you are everything to me. Please don't worry for me. Keep your intelligence focused in the religious principles. I have spent my life with pleasure in your company and now I am prepared to leave it. Please be patient my love."

On listening to his dear wife's words pigeon came down from the tree and came closer to his wife. He was somewhat relieved to see that his wife was still alive. Close to her cage was lying the hunter who was very close to his death as his body was hypothermic and is breathing was very shallow and slow. The pigeon decided to get his wife freed from the cage. He was moving here and there thinking of a plan. But the wife stopped him.

She said "All the relationships in this world are temporary. This cage and my bondage is also temporary. Don't waste your energy and time in freeing me. I don't consider it an offence done by the hunter. This is the fruit of my past karmas only. Please strengthen your intelligence. In any sort of circumstances we must not forget our principals. This hunter is a guest who has come to our home.

"Those people who satisfy the guests visiting their homes with soothing words, they are blessed by goddess Saraswati. Those who feed their guest with good food, satisfy Indra, the God of heaven."

"By washing their feet, we satisfy our elders and by serving them and worshipping them, Lord Vishnu with his wife goddess Lakshmi are satisfied and all demigods are satisfied."

"If after sunset some guest comes who is tired and is hungry, we should think that he has either been sent by the gods or he is one of the gods himself."

"If the guest is pleased that is the reason for biggest happiness. If he goes back sad and dissatisfied, then all demigods and their blessings leave the house."

"So my dear husband please be patient. Don't be disturbed. The real life is the life that is lived for the greater welfare of others."

The husband said "You have said very nice things, but do listen to me. We are just small pigeons how can we serve anyone. Our carrying capacity is only as big as our beaks we can hold. We don't store grains in big urban pots. We have no big stores of water or food what can we do? How can we serve the guests?"

The wife said "We can serve anyone with warmth and fire; some water, sweet words and even some wood which the person can use. All these things can be offered to this hunter who has come as a guest at our home. And now he is being disturbed due to extreme cold, his better clothes and the unfavourable environment. We must serve him anyway we can."

On listening to his wife's sweet words, the he-pigeon went on to the top most branch of the tree. He saw that there was a fire burning at some distance.

He went there and brought a stick from the fire which was still burning at its one end.

He started a small fire near the hunter. He added some twigs and some leaves. Then one by one he kept on putting blades of dry grass and the fire became stronger.

With the heat of the fire the hunter warmed his body.

His freezing body parts now had some life to them.

He felt great comfort.

She-pigeon saw that he was now warm but he was famished.

She said to her husband "My dear husband! Please put the cage and me inside the fire. I will serve this Huntsman in this way as he can fulfil his hunger by eating me after I am dead.

The husband said "This is not your responsibility alone. This is my responsibility too. Being the husband I should be the first one to offer myself to our guest. Please give me permission."

Having said this he remembered Lord Vishnu and other demigods.

He circumambulated the fire three times.

He said to the huntsman "Please use me in your service. After I die you can eat my body and fulfill your hunger."

On seeing this gesture the huntsman's heart started transforming.

Filled with tears, he said aloud "My human body is useless. Because of me this bird has made such a sacrifice that he has left his body."

When he said so, the she pigeon requested him "Please now free me. See my husband is going away from me. I want to follow him."

The hunter got perturbed.

He also got scared witnessing these unimaginable events.

Immediately he freed the bird from the cage.

She circumambulated her husband's body and became ready to enter the fire.

She prayed to the gods and said "It is the greatest honour for a lady to follow her husband on the path of religion. Such a wife is praised in this life as well as the next."

Addressing the hunter, she said "It is because of you that we got this great opportunity. Me and my husband we both are going to the heavenly planets."

After saying this she entered the fire. At that time there was a tremulous sound from the sky.

Jai! Jai! Jai! Jai!

It was the sound of the glorification of the pigeon couple.

Just then a glorious shining golden plane came from the sky.

It was shining like Sun.

The huntsman saw that both the pigeons transformed into two beautiful human forms and climbed that plane.

They said to the huntsman "We are going to the heavenly planets. We need your permission as you are our guest. Your presence came to us as an opportunity to rise on this staircase to the heavens.

As the huntsman saw them going to the higher planets he was amazed.

He threw away the cage, his bow and his arrows.

With folded hands he said "Please don't leave me behind. I am an ignorant person. I have done sins whole my life. Please take me along or give me instructions, how can I be relieved of this life of bondage.

Both of them said "O Huntsman! Our blessings are to you. Please go to the banks of sacred river Godavari. Bow before her and offer all your sins to her. For 15 days, take bath there, thrice a day and follow the topmost religious practices very sincerely."

"Daily say your prayers, remember Lord Vishnu and please him with your service to river Godavari. With dedication and sustained efforts you will be able to please Lord Brahma, Vishnu and Mahesh."

In this way, when you will leave your body there, you will also come to the higher planets. Be assured of that.

The hunter was very satisfied and relieved on listening to the instructions.

He immediately left for the banks of river Godavari and followed the instructions of the divine couple.

He left his past life and all his sins and sinful mentality behind.

In the end he was blessed with a divine life. He was redeemed of the fruit of his hellish actions and was saved from going to hell.

He got liberated.

One who serves becomes the master.

"What do we live for if not to make life less difficult for each other?" – George Eliot, Novelist

The greatest satisfaction comes from helping others.

In this true story, we saw how the two pigeons happily gave their own life to save the life of the hunter.

When we live to serve, our problems seem puny as compared to the greater picture.

We step on the shoulders of our problems and rise above all the atrocious thoughts and disturbing impediments.

*By becoming servants, we become masters;
masters of our senses; masters of our actions;
masters of our fate; masters of our peace.*

*Those who tried to rule turned into grains of
sand. Those who tried to serve are remembered
forever with their names etched with golden
ink in the history of time.*

*Most people in this world live the life of that
hunter, enjoying the power, the control;
thriving on other's fear; making them beg for
their lives.*

*Very few choose to life the exemplary life of
that pigeon couple. But these few people are the
ones who achieve eternal peace and are
remembered for the ages to come*

*Trust me, if its peace that you are looking for,
learn the art of service. Once you make it a
habit, it will create wonders in your life.*

So, what you wanna be?

A master who will end up a deserted hopeless loner or less?

Or a servant who ends up a master of his peace and destiny?

Choice is yours.

VII

Simple living – The Highest Thinking

"That's been one of my mantras – focus and simplicity. Simple can be harder than complex.
- Steve Jobs

We say this often. We preach this more often. We hear this all the time. But do we follow it? Nops.........

Why not? Nobody else is doing it? Not worth doing it? What is the big deal in being simple? Anyone can become that. Being sophisticated holds charm, a mystery is desirable.

All these allurements prevent us from imbibing the most basic virtue of all – Simplicity. Once considered the topmost quality is now looked down upon. It's not trending, it's not hip and it has no value for social fever stuck GenZ.

In an era of brands and showbiz, simplicity has taken a backstage. In the supermarket of demanded attributes, it lies on the lowest shelf with very few takers.

The trend can be seen on as basic platforms as matrimony advertisement. Few years back they used to start with: Wanted a simply girl/boy etc etc. Now this word has gone missing.

As we have lost this word, we have lost our peace.

The stability and serenity in our life has gone fleeting away as our embrace unto simplicity has loosened. Simplicity was the core pillar of every household in India and so was the prevalence of peace.

Want the inner peace back? Imbibe simplicity.

Sharing a simple, thought provoking story from Narsimha Puran which will re-thrust the importance of letting go of pride, ego, position and taking the steps forward on this journey.

Simplicity and peace go hand in hand.

There is no other way.

Eyes of Fire (From Narsimha Puran)

In Madhya Pradesh there lived a brahamin. His name was Kashyap. He was very intelligent, dutiful and expert in scriptural literature and knew the essence of all the known structures and religious books. He was also expert in explaining it to any sort of person. He had his priorities all set and was always one step ahead in full feeling the religion activities and stayed away from non-spiritual activities.

He was also very loving towards his wife. Every morning and every evening he and his wife used to perform fire sacrifice at their home and invited various guests, saints and sages. In this way, they worshipped lord Narsimha.

His wife's name was Savitri. Since she was very devoted to her husband and other household duties, she had special mercy of god on her. She was also very attached to her husband.

Everywhere around she was respected because of her good qualities. In this way both of them were engaged in the path of spiritual enlightenment.

In another part of the state, in a place named Kaushal Desh, there was very intelligent Brahmin whose name was Yagya Sharma and his wife's name was Rohini.

She also was very devoted to her husband and was always ready to serve him. They together produced one son. Yagya Sharma was very pleased to have the son.

He wanted him to be a big support in his journey of spiritual realization. He kept his son's name as Dev Sharma. As he grew older he was taught by his father various spiritual injunctions.

By the time he finished his studies his father left his body. Both mother and son became very sad because of the head of the family leaving this world.

They felt deserted and all alone. But there were great saints around to guide Dev Sharma. They taught him to become patient and stable minded.

One day something stuck his mind and he left his home and started going to all various pilgrimages. He started performing severe austerities.

He tried and controlled his hunger, his sleep and his actions and limited all bodily activities to the minimum.

One day Dev Sharma was taking bath in a river. His clothes were lying on the river bank to dry. He sat on the rock nearby and started chanting the Holy names of Lord on beads.

Just then one crow came and sat on his clothes. Dev in a loud voice shooed him away. The crow flew up. But as he flew up, he excreted on the clothes. Dev got very angry. He saw the bird with the eyes full of anger.

To his surprise the bird in the air caught fire and burnt to the ground. This was an unexpected and unusual site for the sage. Just then another bird, a swan, came close. To stop him, he shouted and saw him with the same looks.

Surprisingly this bird also got burnt to the ground. This was unusual, but in a good way, for Dev.

The sage decided in his mind that it was because of his austerity and difficult lifestyle that he was given this benediction by the God. This pumped up his pride. He started thinking he was special and above all others.

He dressed with clean clothes and went to village to seek something to fill his belly. He used to go every day. But today when he went to the village to ask for alms his walk, his posture and his look was different than usual.

He went to the same village where Savitri was residing. After roaming to few houses he went to the house of Savitri, the chaste and ascetic wife.

He called from the door "O Mother! please give me alms. This sage has come to your door to ask for food and bless you."

Before Savitri could answer his call though they had an eye contact, she remembered that her husband had asked her for some warm water and some other stuff.

So she ran back to first fulfil the desire of her husband. This was difficult to tolerate for Dev Sharma. How she could delay his service. This was an insult to his pride.

Have you ever felt the same? The feeling of insult on being rejected or deprived.

He kept standing at the door burning with fire from the inside. His heart was retching. His lips started trembling.

She served her husband as quickly as possible and came with some food and water at the door to serve this sage.

Dev did not accept it. He just kept looking at her with the same burning eyes with which he had once destroyed the crow and the swan. He kept on looking towards her again and again with the same fierce look but to his disappointment nothing happened.

He was confused. "Why she was not dying?' he was asking himself."

On seeing his face Savitri laughed a little. After a pause she said "O angry sage! I am not that crow or swan who will die because of your anger. If you want this food please accept it with humility and without pride. Otherwise you may leave."

Dev Sharma was taken aback. He did not know what to say or do. He just picked up the food and went away to the place where he used to chant and perform his spiritual activities daily. He sat there, had the food and satisfied his hunger. When Savitri's husband had gone for work, he came back to her house.

He said "O most fortunate lady! I want to ask you something. Please tell me honestly. Who are you? How did you get to know all those events which happened very far from you and in your absence? I worked so hard and lived a painful life to get those powers. You, on the other hand, are a simple household lady. From where did you get this mystic power?"

She replied "I am not a great ascetic like you. I am a housewife and my greatest religion is serving my husband and my family. This is the greatest duty. In day and night, I please my husband so I have got this blessing that I can get to know even what is happening far from here. And that is the reason that I was immune to your burning vision. The effect of your austerities was nullified after you burnt those two birds. Thus, it had no effect on me."

She continued in a grave voice "I want to tell you that after your father passed away, your mother was alone in the village. You should have stayed by her side and helped her in her old age. Instead you came here and now your only concern is fulfilling your own hunger and the futile attempt to gain some mystic power."

She looked him in his eyes and said "Have you ever thought that the lady who gave birth to you, who faced so many troubles to bring you up, you have left her alone in that old helpless stage. Don't you feel ashamed on yourself?"

After saying this, she went silent. Dev Sharma fell on her feet. He was filled with tears of remorse.

He said "O mother! I seek forgiveness from gods for the mistake of killing those birds that I did in ignorance. I did not know my potency. And my greatest offense was when I tried to kill you due to my anger. Please forgive me. Now please tell me what I should do to make my life successful."

Savitri replied "Lead a simple life. Be humble. Keep your anger and unnecessary desire in control. Get married. Produce children. Follow the part of austerity in household life. Serve your mother and help your wife to serve her too. Never speak a lie and lead very serene and peaceful life in this way you will get the success of your life."

The sage Dev Sharma was very thankful to Savitri. He made an instant resolution. "O greatest of the chaste women! I'll go back today to my mother to serve her and protect her. I have kept your talks to my heart. I promise to live a life full of simplicity and without unnecessary desires."

"Leading the life of a sage and controlling my anger, I will worship God in my house to please Him. From today, serving my mother and following the religious principles would be my greatest priority. Thank you so much for opening my eyes."

Dev bowed down to her, accepted her as his spiritual master and went back to his mother. He followed Savitri's instructions, lived his life with simplicity and came to be known as the greatest people of his time.

Simple living – The highest thinking

So true, yet so underrated.

"Nature is pleased with simplicity. And nature is no dummy."- Sir Isaac Newton

"I have just three things to teach: simplicity, patience, compassion. These three are your greatest treasures."- Lao Tzu

"Three rules of work: out of clutter find simplicity. From discord find harmony. In the middle of difficulty lies opportunity."- Albert Einstein

"The core of beauty is simplicity"- Paulo Coelho

Do I need to write more? I feel its enough to convince anyone.

If still not convinced, then Dev is going to come in your dreams with those burning eyes.

Just kidding. LOL

ॐ

VIII
The Final Message

I hope you enjoyed reading this book.

All the qualities described in the book are practical and applicable to all.

I have tried them, lived them and still living them every single day.

Try them. One by one. Make each one of these a habit. You will see miracles happening.

Do give me a feedback of your experience of reading this book and its relevance in your life. You can reach me on hanish.sharma@yahoo.com.

I want to thank you from the core of my heart for giving your time to read this book.

Hare Krsna.